DEstined
DeXdE
DEtermination

DESTINED BY DETERMINATION

Take your De By De!

Take your Destiny into your Own Hands.

You set the Goals,

You make the Plans.

You set the Timeline,

Find resources and tools,

Then EXECUTE!

Restructure, Retool,

EXECUTE!

Do Better, Do More,

EXECUTE!

Every Year, Every Month, Every Week,

EXECUTE!

Every Second, Every Minute, Every Hour,
EXECUTE!

Be DEstined by DEtermination,
Every day take your De By De.

Determination requires a. . .
Focused Sight,
Consistent Breath,
Disciplined Mind and,
Dedicated Steps.

Determination is NOT RESERVED for Good Days!
Be Determined When it's Hard
When it's Rough, When it Hurts, When It Rains.
DETERMINATION ALWAYS!

Be Real with yourself.

Using your current Location,

Keeping it Moving, Rerouting when necessary.

Stay ready for redirection.

DETERMINATION ALL WAYS!

Be DEstined by DEtermination

Take your De By De!

Please be Advised. . .

It takes Work to make this Work.

Diligent Effort,

That's De By De!

There is NO EASY WAY,

No Skipping the New Phase.

That's De By De!

Break it up in Parts and,

Conquer Daily,
That's De BY De!

Work Hard, Do More,
That's De by De!

Save Lives, Get Money,
THAT'S DE X DE

De X De Vol.1: The Willing

Are You Willing To Do The Work?

Author: G'Jurel "G Dash" Jones

Illustrations: by LeRoy Grayson

Publishing: by Jazzy Kitty Publications

DE X DE Vol. 1: The Willing

By G'Jurel "G Dash" Jones

Cover Designed by LeRoy Grayson

Published by Jazzy Kitty Publications

Logo Designs by Andre M. Saunders/Jess Zimmerman

Editor: Anelda L. Attaway

© 2021 G'Jurel "G Dash" Jones

ISBN 978-1-954425-28-6

All rights reserved. This book is protected by the copyright laws of the United States of America. This book may not be copied or reprinted for commercial gain or profit. The use of short quotations or occasional page copying for personal or group study is permitted and encouraged. Permission will be granted upon request. This book is for Worldwide Distribution and printed in the United States of America, published by Jazzy Kitty Publications utilizing Microsoft Publishing Software.

DEDICATION

I dedicate this book to. . .The Willing

                    The Hopeless

                    The Listeners

                    The Conscientious

                    The Fatherless

                    The Parents

                    The Scarred

                    The Accountable

                    The Deficient

                    The Destined

                    The Neglected

                    The Peaceful

                    The Growth

                    The Maintainers

                    The Hungry

                    The Driven

                    The Environmentalists

                    The Procrastinators

                    The Natural

                    The Truthful

The Determined

ACKNOWLEDGMENTS

I thank R.I.P. Jeff Mayo, The Daggets (R.I.P. Aunt Sister and Uncle Stoney), Mr Elmo and Terry Brooks (R.I.P. Jarvis Perry), Donald and Candi Harris (R.I.P. Brent Harris). The Grayson's (R.I.P. Uncle Moses),

Victoria "Knawmean" Jones, Bianca "Cadence" Jones, Frances Jones, Deirdra Jones, Ivy Walters, Ashley Burton, , Bryce, Aston, Christopher, and Baby Aaron. Cindy Jones, Cousins: Jefferson "Jay" Daggett, Lisa, Maurice.

755-7 Granville Butler, Henok Zena, Eddie Santiago, Matt Robinson, Rob Hill Jr., Kevin Shannon,

Sean Kwil Jennings, Maria Duarte, Joanne Quereguan, R.I.P. Theo Mayo

Nate Rhodes, Lindsey Tucker, Harvey Walker, Eldiablo Beckham, D. Pollack, Lisa Ward, Arleen Johnson, Angel Acevedo, Briara Lowery, Chanelle Brock, Jamal Crews, Lenny Williams, Lupe Fiasco, Langston Hughes, Maya Angelou, Martin and Gina Payne.

& Jerry James Jones Jr.

Special Thanks to Jacinta Johnson, Anelda Jazzy Kitty, Leroy Grayson, and YOU THE PEOPLE!

TABLE OF CONTENTS

INTRODUCTION	i
Lord Willin'	iv
Hear's Hope	01
Who's Hearing This	04
Terms and Conditions	11
Since He is Deceased	17
She Sees	20
Time Don't Stop Scars	24
Harsh	28
Point of Reference	32
Reality Scene	38
Their adVantage Point	41
Time Stops	44
Sitting on the Edge of the Past	47
Some Manage	52
Got to Work to Eat	55
My Chauffeur	60
From the Earth	63
Cremation	67
Natural	70
Truth Hurts	77
ABOUT THE AUTHOR	79

INTRODUCTION

Good day, good people. This was written by me as an introspective blessing, lesson, and understandings that I have grown to embody. It is written with the perspectives in mind, meant to inspire growth. These works contain gems I have gathered from my teenage self that I wish I would have known as a youth. These messages also apply to my adult self and appear to have been timeless in my life. I didn't write this as personal therapy but to assist anyone who may need it.

Each poem was written with the understanding that to make it from poverty, you can feel like you are climbing out of an endless hole, especially as a kid who is still trying to understand what life is about. This was written with the thought to preserve that hope when it is hard; you have to be willing and keep the faith. I understand I do not have all the answers, and everything I say will always because I'm just figuring out. I'm human like everyone else. I just try to remember it's okay to be human. I just hope we all grow to understand it is okay to embrace your imperfections, work on your flaws, and celebrate growth throughout the process.

I hope some will Identify and connect this is. I hope this pushes you to keep going regardless of age, race, creed, color, orientation, or any other characteristic of life. This is why I am destined by determination. I understand and will only be able to succeed, but the Lords will or whatever higher power you believe. I am not a religious person, but I am spiritual, and I understand the power of faith. You will wind up stagnant without some sort of belief system.

I am also aware that it is up to us to be willing to grow. It is rather easy to stunt your growth in some situations. There's a bunch of factors that play a part that people don't pay attention to.

A lot of things can happen that people don't necessarily notice or understand. In life, you should always be learning. If you're not learning, you're not living.

That's what this is all about!

Some kids have responsibilities and no one sees them. Things that will affect your success and spread to different areas in life. It's human to have hurt in your upbringing, that and be unaware. These issues may carry through life, and without being checked, can be disastrous to growth or general mental health. As a young Black male raised in the inner city, options feel more limited than they really are. When our viewpoint is restricted, we assume we see things clearly. When you don't know, you really have a clue and you will be in denial for quite some time.

I wrote this is to show that it is possible to make it out. This is also written with the perspective that we get in our own way. I've gotten in my own way too many times to count. I have broken down, failed, and felt lost too many times to count. I have also been blessed and learned countless lessons. When we are in our own way, it is often because we may stand firm in toxic beliefs. We also may not ensure that our actions actually align with our beliefs.

Sometimes we do not admit the existence of our pain. We will deny our own drama and the part we played in it. We will put ourselves in positions that we do not need to be in and justify bad behavior for ego and pride. I had a habit of acting like things are okay when they were not remotely Okay. So much so I convinced myself things were acceptable that were not. I wrote this to address those things so that I can hopefully help others improve. Doing better is definitely not easy, but if you are open, aware, and put in the work, you can, Lord Willing!

LORD WILLIN'

LORD WILLIN' I will be the best!
May God forbid the Opposite.
The World may be Listening. . .

It's Deeper,
My daughters are watching this.
I have to make them. . .
My Sister
And my Mama Proud!

To be more Realistic.
I just need to make sure
My Proud Moments,
Outweigh,
THE DISAPPOINTMENTS!!!

Both are expected when the Love is Consistent
This Life has NO GUARANTEES.

Lessons taught by the man

Who made me

When he didn't care if I was Proud,

Hell, he didn't care to Raise Me!

I know that sounds Harsh,

But be aware Life's Harsh!

Time Heals All Wounds

But it DON'T STOP ~~SCARS~~!

As a child, it was Easy

To write-off Responsibilities.

Became a young adult

Had to work just to Eat.

I REFUSE to Starve headed to my Destination,

I have to take care of Business,

On the Road to Success.

To say it in Laymen's:

I am Driven by Ambition.

I appreciate My Chauffeur!
Contemplating Cremation
I don't want to do Dirt.

I know it's Natural in this World,
We all came FROM THE EARTH.

Patience OVER Procrastination!
So, if this is Painful
I'll Embrace it because. . .
THE TRUTH HURTS!

HEAR'S HOPE

My biggest fear in life has always been the loss of hope. This is because I know when you lose it, it's over. Without hope, it is easy to lose the will to go on. It is highly likely that if you don't have hope, you will not see a future. I have felt like the world would go on without me, and it would not matter. It's a scary place to be. When you feel abandoned, like everyone leaves and nobody cares, you stop caring. That mindset was dangerous and damaged my self-worth at the time, and I didn't even know it. The loss of hope changed my effort, made me cold and hard. When life gets crazy and you don't see the light in your world, it can be easy to slip into depression and not even know it. This is why we have to push through hard and push through consistently. I had to realize that what's happening at the moment is temporary, and right now is not forever. Where you are in life looks different if you look back six months to a year. So, I had to accept that the same would be true if I looked forward six months to a year. Maintaining consistency will bring you to the light on the other side of the struggles. It will always help you to hold onto hope. You do what you have to do to maintain faith. This isn't optional; it's necessary. So, with that who Hears Hope?

DE X DE Vol. 1: The Willing
HEAR'S HOPE

I HOPE the World is HEARING this,

Because I heard HOPE is making appearances,

Where ever you are feeling this,

Reading this

HEARING this.

HEAR'S HOPE

Felt Lost when I Lost it.

Depression distracted my Vision,

NO HOPE in sight.

My HOPELESS HEART needed a North Star.

HEAR'S HOPE

Faith became my Guiding Light.

Hopelessness feels like an Endless Night.

I hope the World is Hearing this

And a Lonely Soul knows

HEAR'S HOPE,

You are not alone in this fight.

You will be Okay!

It will be alright!

So, keep the Faith and hold the Hope tight,

With all your Might, for all your Life!

HEAR'S HOPE

Hope is the Seed that Grows

Into what you Believe.

The Effort is the Water.

The Faith is the Sunlight.

So, I hope the World is hearing this

And Believes in a better Life.

HEAR'S HOPE

Who's Hearing This

So, I've learned that losing is closely connected to feeling unseen and unheard. It gets dark when you only notice the disappoints and you act unaffected by any of it. It's so easy to lose your care for life when you start to feel like everything ends and nobody cares. Then you start to feel like nothing matters and it all goes away anyway. I have found myself thinking about how others view me. Which is only interesting because I simultaneously acted like I didn't care what anyone thought about me. The reality is that legacy lives on through you and after you from the start of you.

Here's a fact: You will disappoint some people, sometimes. It's human. You will also have proud moments often. The disappointing moments will typically feel louder than the proud ones. That does not mean that they are more significant; most of the time, they aren't. They only feel that way because we don't acknowledge the proud moments properly. You are partially defined and will be remembered by both of these moments as a whole. I had to learn the long hard way to just push for a proud moment and try to minimize the casualties of the disappointments. Try not to dwell or fixate on the disappointment. This will only mess with your self-worth and possibly stunt your growth. To busy looking at your issues to look for ways to improve upon them. Just take accountability, look for the lesson and move on. You cannot change what's been done, but you can do better next time. You don't know who's watching, rooting for you, or who you inspire. They may be quiet, or your too busy hearing yourself struggle to hear them cheering for you.

My environment taught me that I should not care what anyone thinks. Boy, was that wrong, not caring what "ANYONE" sounds so extreme at this point. To not care about my family like cousins or auntie's, maybe it possible, but my momma or my sisters or those I consider friends, that is no realistic. Even if I wouldn't admit it to myself but I cared. I need to be aware that I cared. I would notice when someone was disappointed and I clearly didn't like how that felt. I would either be too prideful and convince myself to be unbothered or simply try to ignore them. I still cared, and I was supposed to care. I am human! I am supposed to feel things. I just needed to be selective about who deserved this level of care. I have definitely left good people feeling disconnected and unappreciated because I was too prideful. I dug myself a tunnel from disappointment to depression by not acknowledging the proud moments. I would totally misjudge my impact acting like stuff doesn't matter when it clearly mattered. I was cold, hard, and unhappy. It also made me unable to manage perception. Newsflash, you can't properly manage something you refuse to acknowledge. When people believed in me, I didn't see it because I wasn't looking for it.

I had to learn you really never know who's rooting for you and who you inspire. I have received opportunities from folks I thought didn't notice me, just from being consistent in the right direction. I have had moments where I was barely making it, and someone told me I inspired them. I was like "really? who? where?" I learned just because I didn't think they were listening; doesn't mean they weren't paying attention. I just had to make sure I kept it pushing without allowing myself to be consumed by the validation of people who don't matter. This is all easier said than done. The fact is self-awareness is key and it starts with accepting proud moments and disappointment regardless of Who's Hearing This.

WHO'S HEARING THIS

I hope the World is HEARING THIS.

I know my sister's Watching it

I don't know if my Mom will HEAR THIS

But I know my daughters' Watching it.

So, I hope my Proud Moments

Outweigh my Disappointments

Both are Guaranteed

To Deny, that would be Pointless

I've been Guilty of some Foolishness

Ignorance, Carelessness, Recklessness

I've willfully made Bad Decisions

When I know, I knew better

That's what I hope the World WASN'T Listening

Hoping my daughters were Nonexistent,

Too young to Comprehend it.

Or hopefully, I'm able to make it a Teachable Moment
When I Frame or Reposition it.

Hope my Mama didn't Witness it
Told my sisters and they said, you know better than this
But I WASN'T Listening

Too busy Knowing I was Right
To Admit that I was Wrong
Times when I could Turn it Around
Stop it or at least Slow it Down

Pride says Kept Going until it was Too Far Gone
By the way, this is one way
That Regrets are Born

But
You have to Keep Going
I knew I could Fall Down into the Deep End.

I REFUSE to Drown

The River keeps Flowing, so I might as well

Swim

Life Goes On

Regardless of who's Listening, who's Watching

Regardless of the Disappointments

So, I just hope I have more Proud Moments

I have always Spent More Time

Counting the Bad Times

Then I spent recalling

The times I spent truly Satisfied, Truly Gratified

I need to check the Inventory of my Emotional

Warehouse.

Verify the Vibes.

So, I could Pinpoint

When real Fulfillment was on High Supply

I Know

It doesn't take Major Action to Create

Craters Size Impact

This is not a Problem with Work

Pay attention

You deliver a Smile

Save some Souls

Did you know when you Raise Eyebrows

Somebody Hope

You just gave Somebody Hopes

Take Note of your Achievements

You never know who you're Reaching

You never know who's Listening

Rooting for you

YOU NEVER KNOW WHO NEEDS IT

Terms and Conditions

While you may not be able to control who listens to you or who is watching you. You should be willing to pay attention to who you give your love to. While agape may exist, love is allowed to have conditions, boundaries, and expectations. When you show love, make sure they are qualified to receive it. Be careful about giving yourself to people who don't meet the standard. You can easily lose pieces of yourself. It's okay to be selective and value self-preservation. Nobody can make that selection for you. You should know what you need and what you require in order to give your heart to someone. Be aware other people have their own criteria as well. Understand this, or you may be let down when you learn the hard way. It's not that you don't give out your heart but, you should always have your TERMS AND CONDITIONS.

TERMS AND CONDITIONS

TERMS AND CONDITIONS

Always Exist

Always ask Questions and Check the Fine Print

I was told that Unconditional Love is Real.

I learned of Agape early,

And I guess to Exist

To a Certain Extent.

Just not how it was Explained to me.

I have NEVER SEEN its Presence

And it really only Makes Sense

If it's the parent and a child or Vice Versa.

In Creation, it's the Essence,

But even that I believe

Has its Own Requirements.

THE FACT IS THIS:

To Love and to Be In Love

Can have very Different Requirements.

No one has the Right to Judge

Your Love!

Or the Standards you have before you Receive it.

No one has a Right to Discredit

Your Love!

Only

You,

Need to Believe

You!

Please Beware That YOU. . .

Will probably Fall for Fake Love,

And you will Probably Feel it's Real.

Hell yeah, it Hurts, BUT in Time you will Heal.

You'll Learn that Emotions

And people or Emotional People,

Can be Deceiving,

This may put your Heart on Chill,

Sealed in Steal,

Trying NOT to Feel.

When your Heart needs to be Pampered,

You refuse to be Vulnerable,

And let it be Tampered.

To not be Shattered, as a youth,

It starts with what they DON'T Tell you. . .

Learning Qualifiers,

Reading Expectations,

Knowing Standards,

Be willing to Work if you have Faith in it.

What do you Need to Love?

What do you Need to Be in Love?

Nobody else can give you those answers.

Just know

The feeling may seem to Come and Go

Just know

When it's Real, try to be Healed

From your Damage

To maintain Love, it takes Work.

Consistent Communication

Takes effort for you to Grow together

But otherwise, when you Look into the Eyes,

Of the one you Love,

And they're no longer there

You may try to Hold On to that Love.

Trying to make them to Be Who They Were,

Which Isn't Fair

Now you Don't Love the person That They Are,

You Love the person That They Were.

So, the TERMS AND CONDITIONS of the Love

Is to ALWAYS see them for Who They Are

Embracing them as you Build Together

Knowing the Feeling is Rare.

SINCE HE IS DECEASED

Terms and conditions do not only apply to romantic relationships.

Nothing guarantees that that love, care, or validation will be given, not even from family. I had to be willing to accept that in order to move on. I was told by the world that you're supposed to make your parents proud, but my father was barely in my world. I never knew what would make him proud. When he passed, it was certain that I wouldn't know. He never got to know what would make me proud either. I won't get to ask those questions. I won't get to understand his reasons for neglect. That created anger and emotions I denied, which hurt me. I had to process those feelings. I couldn't just deny it like I didn't care. I had to really accept it for what it was. It's okay to feel the anger, and to be upset. It is necessary to process those emotions; just don't deny them. It took me a long time to accept that pain and move on, especially SINCE HE IS DECEASED.

SINCE HE IS DECEASED

Since my Father is DECEASED

FUCK if he's Proud of Me

Honestly, when he was Alive

The Energy was the Same From Me.

His ONLY Son,

But he ain't Connect to me.

I don't know what made him Proud,

Or what he cared About.

Searched for the Love of my Father,

Daddy Issues were all I found.

When I found out that people who are

Supposed to Care…DON'T.

People who CAN Be There. . . WON'T

Being Alone is Inevitable

Being Cared for is a Variable

They say having a son comes with a sense of. . .

PRIDE.

Before I could ask him why,

he didn't develop that Sense of Pride,

At any point in time.

Throughout my 15 yrs. Of Life. . .

HE DIED.

On his Death Bed,

He set some time aside for my sisters.

He didn't care about his ONLY Son's. . .

PEACE OF MIND.

So, if I should Care Now,

About if I would have made him Proud.

Somebody got to tell me why?

THAT'S DEAD!

SHE SEES

When you don't have an active father in your life, you begin to talk to yourself a little differently. You question some things differently, especially when you have a child. You have to be willing to do some things that you have never seen or done before. You have to be willing to be vulnerable and uncomfortable at times. You have to know that child is looking for you as an example of how to live life. You have to move a little differently because they're learning from you. I know my daughters see how I am regardless of how I feel about it. So, I have to be mindful.

At the time, I have to put myself to the side and do the best no matter how annoying or how rough or frustrating it may be. I had to be aware that SHE SEES.

SHE SEES

I've really got to Watch myself

Watch my Words

Watch what I Do

Watch My Vibes and how I Move

My Internal Mood and External Attitude

Perception thinks the world's Watching

Awareness knows my Lil Girls Watching

Learning something from Everything

Taking Mental Notes is a Constant.

When I Cause and Solve Problems,

I pour out some Knowledge.

When flooded with Biased Emotions

It Spills, and she there, Sippy Cup in hand like…

"DADDY, I GOT IT"

Ignoring that Reality is NOT an option.

So, I've got to Watch myself,

She has a Clear View,

If I Appreciate the Wins,

Find a Lesson when I Lose.

SHE SEES

What I allow my World to,

Accept and Approve or Reject and Remove

SHE SEEPS

When I Reflect the world's Honesty,

Or Project my Living Truth

SHE SEES

If the Frustration of Failure is followed by Resilience.

If Gratifying success is followed by Contentment.

How I react when dealing with,

Regrets and Resentment

My Sins in Conjunction with my Repentance,

While seeking Redemption

SHE SEES IT!

I really got to watch myself.

TIME DON'T STOP SCARS

I understand that what my daughter sees from me will carry with her through life. This made me understand that what I have seen and been through, I'm carrying with me throughout life. Whether I like it or not. I had to be willing to embrace and understand those issues so that I don't recreate those generational curses with my children. My daddy was an alcoholic, I saw family members be committed and I had crackheads outside my front door. These things affected my perspective be a little and my life a lot. I had to become aware of that too kind of move past it, otherwise, I would always be haunted. I had to truly understand that TIME DON'T STOP SCARS.

G'Jurel Jones
TIME DON'T STOP SCARS

They say Time Heals All Wounds
But it DON'T STOP SCARS.

Just because you CAN'T see Blood
Don't mean the Pain is Gone.
Just because I Clean up Well
Don't mean I'm Internally Healed

Some wounds Closed, Scabbed and Sealed
But it will NEVER Heal
It NEVER Leaves.

I feel it Vividly in my Memory
And I ETERNALLY Grieve.
It's so hard to stop Generational Wounds
FROM SCARRING ME.

It's Hereditary Personally and Systemic for Society.

When situations Scratched my Soul,

Scraped my Spirit,

Snatched my Smile,

And Stole my Innocence

These SCARS sing to the Tune

Of a Jailhouse Tattoo,

Or more like a Hot Branding Iron

If you let it Label you.

Either way, it don't just Go away,

I just act like it don't affect me.

You can hear the Struggle

If you get close enough as I Convey

With a Cadence set to the Rhythm of the Murmur

In my Cold Purple Heart.

I hope this helps me heal.
I can't just Chill
And be glad that I didn't Bleed out,
Hurt people Hurt people, and I got kids.

I can't have them spending life gathered around
As Pass the Pain out,
With the same Knife that was used
To cut my light out.

Generational wounds
Leaving family SCARS Disguised as Heirlooms.

See, if you have been Traumatized when you Survive
The SCARS keep the Pain Alive,
Because any given Glance
You will Relive that Pain every time.
TIME HEALS ALL WOUNDS.
ONLY IF U HAVE TIME!

HARSH

I understood that generational curses are real. Those harsh lessons that you wind up living through cause certain issues in life. It would be wrong to act like that's the sole reason for some of my faults. In order to be better as a human being, I had to be willing to take accountability.

I have to take accountability for my fault and flaws in order to fix them, regardless of where they came from. I haven't always been the best human being. I haven't always made the best decisions. I've hurt people's feelings before and walked away carelessly. I haven't always been honest, respectful, or caring. I definitely wasn't as always as great of a person as I thought I was.

I have to take accountability for that and it's not always easy being that brutally honest with yourself. If you can Embrace those things, then you can work on them and be a better human being. That's not always nice, in fact, sometimes, it's downright HARSH.

HARSH

Warning: This will sound HARSH, but I don't care

Life is HARSH.
Where should we Start
You Fucked Up; you were all the way wrong,
Yes, it is ALL YOUR FAULT

Sometimes you're Selfish
And you Lack Communication
Sometimes you're Neglectful
And you Lack Consideration

You have Overinflated your Greatness,
Let your Arrogance Glaze
Your Unrealistic Expectations

Creating Preventable Insecurities
That Self-sabotage your Self-esteem

And sometimes you just DON'T work hard enough,

NEWSFLASH

Most of the time, nobody gives a Fuck.

Not enough to be Active or show Real Support.

you are really not that significant

SO WHAT

WHO CARES

TO BE FAIR,

You don't Think or Pray when you say

"You're sending thoughts and prayers."

Yes, this sounds HARSH, but Nobody Cares

The fact that you Love them,

Doesn't mean they WON'T Use you.

The fact that they are around

Doesn't mean they Choose you

The fact that you care

don't mean they have to care too

SOOOO. . . they probably don't care about you.

You probably shouldn't care as much as you do

Time DON'T STOP so almost everyone is Expendable

You have Misled and you have been Lied to.

You have Trivialized, Rationalized,

And Justified a Bunch of Mess

Look in the Mirror and Tell the Truth

You be on some BULLSHIT!

Point of Reference

Those harsh reflections come from a place of self-love. Which took me way too long to figure out. Then I thought about how I learned what love is, be it self-love, loving others, all those things. That can be such a hard one to figure out. Learning how do you properly provide love.

In order to figure that out, you have to be willing to understand what it looked like for you. Think about how you saw it in life growing up. I didn't have it around consistently in the home, so I learned from TV. You should recognize that where your view of love comes from. That's when you can create your own standard and create your own understanding of what love is and what it looks like. It is important to know your Foundation and knowing your POINT OF REFERENCE.

POINT OF REFERENCE

When you're Illiterate to Love Languages,

It's hard to understand Love's Lessons.

Citing the sources of the Heart,

It's hard to find a POINT OF REFERENCE.

None inside the Home.

Shouts out to The Brooks, The Smiths,

And The Harris's.

A few inside the family,

The Grayson's:

The Daggets.

How do you Learn that Love

Is something more than a Weakness?

How do you learn that you need it,

And how to express it?

When I only saw it every now and then

Here is my POINT OF REFERENCE
The way Cliff LOVED Claire Huxtable
Was Phenomenal!

They were Five Kids Deep
And Completely removed from Poverty.

So, I don't know how they got there.
I don't know what they went through
So, to a Little Black Boy in the Hood,
That's NOT Relatable or Attainable.

Here's my POINT OF REFERENCE
I love the way James LOVED Florida Evans
To see him Embracing her Natural FRO,
Loving the Gap Infatuated with her Imperfections.
That Love was Impressive!

He NEVER had Peace,

always struggling, always yelling.

And they started off with them being three kids in.

So, I don't know how they got there.

Where did the Love begin?

How does the Love begin?

Next POINT OF REFERENCE

Uncle Phil and Aunt Viv

They watered down her Melanin and quite quick

And Diluted her Sassy-ness.

Yes, they were Rich and three kids in.

No, I could NOT RELATE.

At the time all, I was Attracted to women

Who wanted the Smoke

I don't know how they Fell in Love.

Was he already a Judge on the First Date?

Next POINT OF REFERENCE

Martin and Gina

I guess that's the Closest to Reality.

I mean, he wasn't Sweet for NO REASON

Only Vulnerable when he had to be.

Pride almost Cost him his woman a few times.

That was Real, or at least that's how it seems.

So, Martin was the most consistent

POINT OF REFERENCE of L O V E for me.

Sheesh!

Thinking being with the woman of my Dreams.

More than Sleeping with her.

Didn't know how to Cherish, Have and Hold.

Those are Vows I didn't consider.

What do you do with Love. . .Real Love?

The Kind of Love that made Adam give a Rib
Reconsider read some Literature on the Subject!
He did it for Companionship.

That's because it takes more than Love,
But Nobody tells you this.
They make it seem like it should be Effortless.
Talk to those who have made it. . .

They will say it take Endurance, Patience, Compromise,
And Communication.

You have to Learn the Language,
To Comprehend the Lesson.
Know the sources of your Standards,
And understand your POINT OF REFERENCE!

Reality Scene

After examining my point of reference for love and life in general, I had to accept what I'm becoming. I had to accept that this life isn't random. Cause and effect is real. Even if the effects don't take place today or tomorrow, they can take place whenever down the line. That's how life works, whether we like it or not. A lot of things are based upon the decisions that we make. Even reality shows are guided or often scripted; most people just don't know it. The way life is you can write your own script. You can build your future.

I had to be willing to accept that what I do in this moment will affect me and others. This includes people I may not know. This life that we live in is not a REALITY SCENE.

REALITY SCENE

Some people would Love to Believe that this Life is. . .

An amazing Game of Risk.

Where you at War with yourself on this Floating Sphere

Where Anger, Hatred, and Fear

Provide consistent attempts to Sink,

Your Mental Battleship.

I don't know if that's it.

I mean, it may have Elements.

I just don't know if we need something more.

The consistent Cause and Effect

Of History Repeating itself,

Until Growth is Achieved,

Thru change,

Or

Self is Destroyed

By Addicting Tendencies

Not always Related to a Drug,

Sometimes related to being

A Human Being

This World lives somewhere

Between a Beautiful Nightmare

And a Stank Looking Dream.

Reality seems to NOT be a Reality Scene.

Their adVantage Point

The same way that I can affect others' reality, others can affect my reality. The People who have the most power can affect your reality based upon their own agenda.

I had to be willing to accept that I have to be consistent in my own actions. This is because they will analyze me, they will tear me down, and limit my growth. The efforts to make me a statistic because if I'm a number, I'm a lot easier to manage. So, because I know what they will do based on their own agenda, powerful people and prominent people live in a place of narcissism often.

They'll do whatever to the common person, especially a person of color, in order to reach their goals. Without caring about the perspective of anyone else. It's all about their hitting THEIR ADVANTAGE POINT.

THEIR ADVANTAGE POINT

Assumptions of the Unaffected

That don't care for the Neglected.

Opinions of the Ill-informed.

Hoping to Redirect the Disrespected.

That's easier than to Face it.

They would rather throw Feces on the Faces,

Of the Disenfranchised until they are Faceless.

Then Label them Ain't Shit.

Ignorance is Systemic the Hatred is Deliberate.

The Inconsiderate are so Rigid

Don't Know

Don't Show

Don't Care

So, they DON'T Get it.

The Pretentious just don't admit it,

Because of their Network or Finances,

Are Elevated compared to the Public,

Or at least that's how they Portray their Image.

But when we Make it Out,

It makes them Livid.

Can't simulate Discrimination, Poverty, Entitlement,

Or Privilege

Or the Effect that these Intangibles

Have on our Prideful Egos,

Self-worth, Value, Awareness, and Image.

Dammit!

When ignorance has the ADVANTAGE

I'm just another nigger. . .that's it.

Now ask yourself. . .

How are you demeaned by their decisions?

. . .I'm finished!

Time Stops

This is heavy. You know, dealing with influences in your world and personal accountability be overwhelming. It can feel like you're are drowning while on your path. I had to be willing to accept that you can't be on go mode all the time. Take a breath; it's okay to feel and enjoy life.

I find that the best times are when you can enjoy someone's company and it feels like you are the only two on earth. Through great conversation, taking a walk, or listening to music, that's where you can feel free. You are able to truly relax when the moment makes TIME STOP.

TIME STOPS

I Love how it Feels when TIME STOPS

When you Got me

I got You and we're ALL We Need

And Forever is ALL We Got

While my Arms are Around you

When your Head is on my Chest

While I Protect my Peace

That Security Guard can rest.

We are at our Best

In Moments like this.

All we Hear is the…

Song being Sung by the Sea

The earth Intertwined our Energy.

This Sits in our Destiny.

DE X DE Vol. 1: The Willing

The World ONLY belongs to us

We ONLY Feel each other's Presence

I Love that TIME STOPS,

When we Enjoy each other, Essence

Sitting On the Edge of the Past

In those moments, please breathe and enjoy life. Appreciate that you made it this far.

I didn't start celebrating my birthday until I was about 21. I only did it because I knew that on paper, based on the world's assessment of me, I should have been dead or in jail. That's when I decided that I'm going to celebrate every year of life that I am not what they said I would be. I had to reflect because we spend so much time focused on the negativity that we don't always recognize our growth. You have to be willing to see how far you've made it. This is even if you've only made it in an inch farther than where you began in this world. That way, you can smile looking forward while you're SITTING ON THE EDGE OF THE PAST.

SITTING ON THE EDGE OF THE PAST

One the Edge of the Bed

Pen and Pad in my Hand

Close my Eyes and See the Past

Now I Smile, then I Laugh.

Ironically relieved that I'm still here

After all, I've Lost and all I've Grieved

High Risk of the Penitentiary

Blood Lost on the Street,

Blood Left on the Leaves.

Pen and Pad in my hand,

Knowing I REFUSE to Write

AWAY my Past.

Until my eyes see the times

When I Denied my Cries

And Internalized my Sad

Pen and Pad in my hand,

Trying to find a way,

To write AWAY the Depression

On the Edge of my Bed,

I Sit, Smile now I Laugh,

Close my Eyes see my Past.

The Sight of who I was

Makes me Proud of who I am,

Life's journey gets Dark sometimes,

But I Embrace where it began

Pen and Pad in my Hand,

As I ask the Write way,

If I'm on the Right Path.

On the Edge of my Bed,

I Sit, Smile, and I Laugh,

Until I Flash to the Moments,

When I long for what I NEVER had

I'd Express it as Anger

And it STILL makes me Mad.

Pen and Pad in my Hand,

As I ask how long I will have

The Write to be Mad.

On the Edge of my Bed,

Open my Eyes

Smile and Stand.

Then I keep it Moving with

Take the Lessons as Blessing

And Appreciate the Past.

Conquering the World

Or at least Reaching Success

Whatever that Success is for you Starts with

Wanting More and Wanting Better.

You have to be Willing to

Want something Different.

It really is Mental.

I raised Section 8

And had Great Times in Poverty.

I have definitely used EPT

To purchase Expensive Seafood.

Why not?

I also know that I don't want to be defined

By those Moments of my Life.

Some people can be Content in that Space

And Living that way for the Rest of Their Days.

I'm not Judging; there's nothing wrong with that.

If that's what you Want, have a Blast!

Just know in Order to Achieve more

You have to Want More

Regardless of how SOME MANAGE

Some Managed

Conquering the world or reaching success, whatever that success is for you, starts with wanting more, and wanting better. You have to be willing to want something different. It really is mental. I was raised in section 8, and had great times in poverty.

I have definitely used EPT to purchase expensive seafood. Why not?

I also know that I don't want to be defined by those moments of my life. Some people can be content in that space and living that way for the rest of their days. I'm not judging; there's nothing wrong with that. If that's what you want, have a blast! Just know in Order to achieve more, you have to want more ,regardless of how SOME MANAGE.

SOME MANAGE

I've seen SOME MANAGED to walk through life

Cashless

That's something I don't get.

For me, that Shoe Don't fit.

I seen it

People permanently pushing through Poverty

Saying

"We managing."

"We makin' it."

"We getting by."

When Survival is the State of Mind

Limited is the Fate.

No Goals to be Great

Mediocre Mind State

Ambition gone WITHOUT a Trace

No Cash, Credit, or Coin

Now Crypto, No Bit.

Scheming for endless Medicaid, EBT, and WIC.

Look if that's what you do. . .

Solid, do you.

But the way I Move

I'll be Tripping if I Choose,

To Walk in those Shoes.

I ain't with it,

I'm trying to collect. . .

Currency, Raise Decimals and Digits.

So sick of Survival

I will Manage what it takes be Momentous!

Got to Work to Eat

That will nourish and its process, so here's the thing. A lot of people say that they just want to eat and they can't wait to get it. The question is, are they willing to do the work. Once they are able to have a decent meal, please pay attention to what goes into it. All food ain't good food. It's not easy to watch what you eat. I'm talking about not just financially; I'm talking about everything that you're putting into your system. It's not just about how to acquire what we want. It's also about if what we want is good for us. Simply put in order to try to live a healthy life, it's more the gaining nourishment. Always remember you GOT TO WORK TO EAT.

GOT TO WORK TO EAT

Rents due on the first GOT TO WORK GOT TO EAT

Those who Refuse to do the work

Silently show the will except a Lower Quality.

Some are meant to Eat what they Kill

Some stomachs get Weak.

Loss Taste Raw!

It makes you Nauseous

When you CAN'T Process

Read research, do the Math, Take Notes, Do the Work.

Prepare the Meal

Or Prepare to Pay someone else to do it.

You know there's Value in the Work placed into it

When what's your Eating is Unseasoned

It tends to Miss the Cultural Flavor

Simple Google Search can change your Life, Player.

That's all it really takes

To generally verify what you're taking in

Nutrition Facts on your Brain Food

You must do the Work to Verify the Knowledge

Before you take it in.

Self-care

YOU GOT TO WORK GOT

BECAUSE YOU GOT TO EAT

How are your Mental Meals Prepared?

Too Many Cooks in the Kitchen

Voices in your Ear.

The Work

Sustain yourself

Know yourself so you can help yourself

Come Up for Air

When it comes to self-care

Being there

I just want to eat

Spiritual Food to Protein Shakes

Watch Your Intake

Pay attention to Everything you Take

And assess the source of someone that says

"You don't have what it takes."

To be great in your own way.

Don't pay the attention,

It will cost for them to make

The Food on your Plate.

Discipline is on the List

It's Work to Show Restraint.

It takes time

It would be Well Worth the Wait

Takes Patience to Eat

Whether you Prepare it

Collaborate

Or you work to Pay for someone else to Create.

PREPARE TO WORK

Chauffeur

Did I mention that it won't be easy? You have to put in work and it has to be consistent.

So, when you don't feel like it and don't want to, you have to push through. Those are the times when that ambition matters so much more. The drive is what allows you to progress.

You must be willing to understand what moves you. Please don't forget what pushes you what drives you to greatness. Always remember to appreciate your CHAUFFEUR.

CHAUFFEUR

Driven by ambition, I appreciate MY CHAUFFEUR

Dreams feel my Vision

That's my Engine

Every Cylinder

Custom pumps to push me towards my purpose

Shocks done

So, I don't just Bounce

But my System is Nervous

On my way to my Location

Predetermined Destination

Destined by the Determination

My motivation that's the Battery in my Back

Reset and Recharge.

Repurposing the Head

Remembering the Potential in my Power is Great

Making sure I know

How far I've Come

How far I can Go

Get some sleep,

Watch what I eat

Then you can Come Back Tomorrow.

CHARGED UP

From the Earth

Something that is that is severely underrated is taking care of yourself and your environment.

It's a major issue that goes unaddressed and often unnoticed in many communities. I wasn't properly taught, at least not consistently, how to take care of myself mentally or how to take care of the environment. I make plenty of mistakes and don't address things the way I should. Nobody's perfect. It starts with awareness. We will actively do stuff that can kill the environment like we don't live here. Then do stuff that will harm our mind and can destroy our mental health. We do these things like we won't need our brains and we won't need peace. Then we won't make all these things right just because it's easier not to think about them. We have to make sure we take care of ourselves. Be willing to put in the effort to try to take care of yourself and try to take care of your world. We all came FROM THE EARTH.

FROM THE EARTH

We all came FROM THE EARTH

Made FROM THE EARTH

Since Birth

Somehow the message to take care of ourselves

And the EARTH

Got Buried in the Dirt

This isn't a Message about Air Emissions.

A Message for you to take care of what helps you.

Understanding the Value of the Air you Breathe

To be Lost in the Fog

Realize

This isn't how it's supposed to be

Normalizing the Wrong things

When doing things the Right way,

Sound Strange.

Taking care of Yourself
And your Mental Health
Getting Rid of your Pain.
Finding a Place of Peace.

Understanding it Lives inside
You can Kill the EARTH with the Energy you bring
Understanding your Impact is Real.
Those that surround you should understand
That it matters.

The Water
That will leave you Nourished
Or Drown you

Sometimes you have to Embrace the Rain
Dehydration is the Alternative
Don't welcome the Opposite.

We all came FROM THE EARTH

So on to the EARTH

We should Give. . .

To Each Other, we should Give

To Ourselves, we should Give.

AS LONG AS WE LIVE.

Cremation

Here's a fun fact part of maintaining your drive and motivation: You have to be willing to burn it all down if you need to. In order to keep certain things going, you have to walk away from others. I have definitely stayed in situations and did dirt because I didn't want to be there. Then I am justifying bad behavior. Sacrificing morality or lacking Integrity because I'm in a situation that I don't want to be in. Typically, a situation I should have already burned down. Times when you take too long to, you'll wind up losing yourself or losing your motivation.

The fact that you're not where you want to be and you haven't taken those necessary steps can become exhausting. Doing this takes attention away from your own growth and success.

As far as when to walk away, you have to come to that conclusion on your own in order to grow and maintain peace. Sometimes we all know when it's dead and it's time for CREMATION.

CREMATION

CONTEMPLATING CREMATION,

I DON'T want to do Dirt

So, I'm sitting and thinking it's ALREADY Messed up

You might as well let it Burn

If you Stay, you will need to do MORE than Pray

When you do Walk Away

It'll Be Too Late

Say sometimes you got to

CONTEMPLATE CREMATION, Set it ALL on Fire

Because you don't. . .

You will Lose EVERYTHING that keeps you Inspired

You will Die inside yourself

Hate what you have Become,

Be Angry that you DIDN'T Walk Away

Now It's Too Late to Run

You better off Letting it Burn
CONTEMPLATE HOW TO CREMATE
Because its Ashes to Ashes and Dust to Dust
I DON'T want to do Dirt
Because that could just be a Waste

I understand and Try to Biodegrade
This Energy Recycled
What I have Right Now
I need to do more than Save

I need to Preserve
I need to Set Boundaries of what this can be. . .
Within this Stage,

Time within this Space

What I'm Trying to Say
So, you DON'T do Dirt
Sometimes you gotta CREMATE

Natural

In order to manage your mental health, you have to be willing to accept that it's natural to feel things. We are all human. I've had moments where I internalized my emotions because I did not think it was okay to have emotions. I did not know how to express myself. Honestly, I didn't even know what I was feeling, or that I even felt anything.

Life got uncomfortable. I couldn't even move past the hurt. You can't move past certain things until you accept them. You know, in order to get out of some dark places, you have to choose to feel and express that you are in those places. I encourage you to find your avenue of expression. Whether it is writing, playing sports, sewing, or just taking walks. Own it put it into action. Whatever it is for you, that avenue to express your emotions often.

The world may not want you to express your truth but, if you need to do what you got to do for you. No matter what, like it or not needing expression and having feelings are NATURAL.

NATURAL

It's NATURAL that Everything that's Good

To you

Is NOT Good FOR you

It's NATURAL

Not Normal

In this World.

Where they will Silence you for Speaking your Truth.

It's NATURAL in the World where what's Normal

Is defined by those who's…

Self-esteem is Low

Practices are Unusual

But in front of you

What they do

Is NOT Acknowledge you

Or Based on the Position

They say you're NOT NORMAL

So, it's NATURAL

To feel Out of Place sometimes

It's NATURAL

To feel Lost sometimes

It's NATURAL

To have to Figure it out

It's NATURAL

To want Growth and Change

It's NATURAL

To be you

NOT Replicated

We are NOT the same

It's NATURAL

To have Fears

It's Detrimental

To Let them Control you

It's NATURAL

To be Passionate

It's Dangerous to NOT have Levels

It's NATURAL

To see Dark Places

Destructive to live in them

It's NATURAL

To take a Loss Hard

It's Destructive

To NOT Celebrate your Wins

It's Destructive

To NOT Learn from both of them

Internalize your Pain

For Fear of Judgement

It's NATURAL

To Feel Pain.

Normal,

To Internalize.

The Pain

And Fear of Judgment

I say that again

It's NATURAL

To Feel Emotions

It's NATURAL to Feel Pain

NATURAL to feel fear

NATURAL to feel happiness

It's NATURAL to express

It's Normal to Internalize

Whatever

You've been Conditioned to Believe,

As if free thinking

Deserves Disrespect

Whatever

You've been Conditioned to Believe

Will be

Treated as if it should be

Done with the Regret.

It's NATURAL

To find Peace

Within yourself

It's Normal

For people to try to take

Your Peace in this World

It's NATURAL

When you find your Peace

For you to Keep your Peace,

For you to Protect your Peace.

If you DON'T Believe

Any given time

In the place where

Emotions are Screaming

You'll hear the Peace

Is there NATURAL Peace?

Truth Hurts

I Cut Deep

Let It Bleed

For you to See

What has made me

I Cut Deep

Let It Bleed

For you to Read

What has Saved me

Sometimes in order to

Help heal others

I have to show

What moves thru the veins of me.

You have to Cut Deep

Let It Bleed

Because the TRUTH HURTS

Sometimes to help others

A little Pain is all we need

ARE YOU WILLING?

ABOUT THE AUTHOR

G'Jurel Jones is poet, writer, motivator and father of two little girls who was raised out of poverty and struggle. I was able to find my voice through music and poetry in my teenage years. As my sister provided my musical and poetic influences, I felt a deep connect to them. I also recognized the power of the pen. This connection grew with me. The skills developed in to more than a form of expression but also a way to help others. I believe that being destined by determination allows us to prosper if we are willing to do the work.

As I grew, I learned my purpose in life is to conned people to information and understanding. Before I knew this purpose, I made a song with Eddie Santiago, that encompassed many of the life lessons I learned throughout my adulthood. These lessons were based on things I wish I learned earlier life. After understanding my purpose, I wanted to break that song down further and share these lessons, within hope to help other misguided teens, troubled adult, or any one in the general public. I became determine to make it my destiny. I broke the song down by verse, This book is the first verse. The song was titled Lord Willin'.